THE SOUNDS OF EARTH

Side 1

NASA

UNITED STATES OF AMERICA
PLANET EARTH

VOYAGER'S
GREATEST HITS

VOYAGER'S
GREATEST HITS

THE EPIC TREK
TO INTERSTELLAR SPACE

ALEXANDRA SIY

Charlesbridge

To Vicki Cobb—

dear friend, mentor, and the Voyager 1
of children's nonfiction literature

Photo Credits
Cover: ESA/Hubble & NASA/JPL-Caltech, endsheets: NASA/JPL, i: NASA/JPL, ii–iii: NASA, v: NASA/JPL, vi: ESA/NASA, 2–3: NASA/JPL-Caltech/UCLA, 4: NASA/Marshall Space Flight Center, 8: NASA/JPL, 10: NASA, 12: NASA, 14: NASA/JPL, 15 and 16: re-created from the drawings of Galileo Galilei, 18: NASA/Carla Cioffi, 19: NASA/JPL, 21 (inset): NASA/JPL, 21 (background): NASA/JPL/USGS, 24: NASA/JPL, 26: NASA/JPL, 27: NASA/JPL, 28 (left and right): NASA/JPL, 32: NASA/JPL-Caltech, 34: NASA/JPL/USGS, 35: NASA/JPL, 36: Diane M. Earley, 38: NASA/JPL, 40: NASA/JPL, 44: NASA/JPL, 45: NASA/JPL, 46: NASA/JPL/USGS, 47: Lars Mejnertsen and Imperial College London 2015, 48: NASA/JPL, 51: NASA/SDO/AIA, 53: NASA, 56: NASA/JPL-Caltech, 58: NASA/JPL-Caltech, 62: NASA/JPL, 63: NASA/JPL, 64: ESA/Hubble & NASA, 67: Alexandra Siy

Published by Charlesbridge
85 Main Street
Watertown, MA 02472
(617) 926-0329
www.charlesbridge.com

Library of Congress Cataloging-in-Publication Data
Names: Siy, Alexandra.
Title: Voyager's greatest hits: the epic trek to interstellar space/by Alexandra Siy.
Description: Watertown, MA: Charlesbridge, 2017.
Identifiers: LCCN 2016013223 (print) | LCCN 2016021094 (ebook) |
    ISBN 9781580897280 (reinforced for library use) |
    ISBN 9781607349556 (ebook) | ISBN 9781607349563 (ebook pdf)
Subjects: LCSH: Planets—Exploration. | Outer space—Exploration. | Voyager Project.
Classification: LCC QB601 .S59 2017 (print) | LCC QB601 (ebook) | DDC 523.4—dc23
LC record available at https://lccn.loc.gov/2016013223

Printed in China
(hc) 10 9 8 7 6 5 4 3 2 1

Display type set in Croteau by Typodermic
Text type set in Adobe Caslon Pro by Adobe Systems Incorporated
Color separations by Colourscan Print Co Pte Ltd, Singapore
Printed by 1010 Printing International Limited in Huizhou, Guangdong, China
Production supervision by Brian G. Walker
Designed by Diane M. Earley

Half title: Wide-angle farewell shot of Uranus taken by Voyager 2 on January 25, 1986.

Full title: Artist's rendering of Voyager 1 traveling through interstellar space.

Opposite: The first-ever image of both Earth and Moon, taken by Voyager 1 from 7.25 million miles (11.66 million kilometers) out.

CONTENTS

ADVENTURE OF A LIFETIME

TRACK 1

The year is 1990, and Voyager 1 is speeding through space at 39,000 miles per hour (17.43 kilometers per second). Its camera has been turned off for ten years in order to save power and memory for future exploration.

But the urge to look back and take one last glance at home is irrepressible. So on February 14 the camera aboard Voyager 1 is turned on for a few minutes. From 3.7 billion miles (59.5 billion kilometers) out, Voyager 1 snaps sixty photos to make the most distant portrait of the solar system ever. It is a valentine from outer space.

The image of planet Earth is so small it is easily missed: a "pale blue dot" in a vast void. But the message is clear. It is a note to humanity, signed in a sunbeam: *Take good care.*

To the stars

The Voyager Planetary Mission began in 1977, when the twin spacecraft Voyager 1 and Voyager 2 were launched on a four-year tour to Jupiter and Saturn. They reached Jupiter in 1979 and Saturn in 1980 and 1981—but the mission did not end there. In 1986 Voyager 2

The Voyagers are the first explorers from Earth to leave our solar system and enter interstellar space. (Image of star cluster NGC 290 by Hubble Space Telescope, 2004.)

made it to Uranus, and in 1989 it observed Neptune. On January 1, 1990, with all the planets behind the Voyagers, the mission was extended one more time. It became the Voyager Interstellar Mission (VIM). Its new goal: to explore the space between the stars. Humanity's interstellar age had begun.

Cruising north at 38,000 miles per hour (17 kilometers per second), Voyager 1 entered interstellar space on August 25, 2012. Traveling along a southern route at about 34,000 miles per hour (15.4

kilometers per second), Voyager 2 is close behind. The Voyagers are explorers in a new frontier, collecting data and revealing the unexpected. The discoveries they're making on their one-way ticket out of the solar system are helping scientists rewrite the astronomy books.

But wait—not so fast, Voyagers! You can't look back, but we can. All the way back, to the beginning.

A long time ago, in a galaxy called the Milky Way, there was a rare planetary alignment, a cool idea, and a tiny bit of computing power.

A huge section of the Milky Way galaxy, imaged by NASA's WISE (Wide-field Infrared Survey Explorer) telescope.

THING 1 AND THING 2

It's 1965, and the Beach Boys are singing about California girls. Over in Pasadena a graduate student named Gary Flandro is studying aeronautics at Caltech. Gary also has a part-time job: not flipping burgers, but investigating missile trajectories at NASA's Jet Propulsion Lab (JPL). This is literally rocket science. When Gary's boss suggests he might also think about gravity-assist rocket trajectories to the outer planets, Gary is psyched.

MR. SPACEMAN

Unlimited, gravity-propelled interplanetary space travel had been invented four years earlier by Michael Minovitch, a graduate student studying physics and mathematics at UCLA.

Michael knew that the gravity of a planet could affect the path of an object flying by it. This idea was not new. In the early 1800s astronomers looked through their telescopes and discovered that the orbit of a comet flying by Jupiter changed ever so slightly. Clearly, Jupiter's immense gravity influenced the path of the comet.

Voyager 1 was launched on September 5, 1977, aboard a Titan III-Centaur rocket.

What *was* new was Michael's idea of using gravity to propel a spacecraft from one planet to the next, indefinitely. Using mathematics and the latest IBM computers, Michael showed how the spacecraft could get a boost—an "assist"—from the gravity of the planet. It could "steal" some of the planet's speed and accelerate away from the Sun without using even one more drop of rocket fuel! Of course, nothing in the universe is free. The motion of the planet would be affected a tiny bit. Jupiter, for example, would slow down at a rate of 12 inches (30 centimeters) in a trillion years—but the passing spacecraft would speed up by 36,000 miles per hour (16.1 kilometers per second). Just like in a tug-of-war, the big kids win while the little kids go flying.

In the early 1960s, fast and powerful computers were expensive and huge. The IBM personal computer (PC) wouldn't be invented for another twenty years. Michael did all of his computing on the giant IBM 7090-7094 computers owned by JPL and UCLA. His programs sometimes ran for more than ten hours at a time, so he had to work on weekends and late at night when the computers were not in use by other researchers. Michael showed that a spacecraft could fly from Earth to Venus, to Mars, back to Earth, then on to Saturn, then all the way to Pluto, then back to Jupiter, and finally back home, without using any more rocket fuel than what it took to get to Venus in the first place. The spacecraft would literally be falling through space from one planet to the next.

SLINGSHOT IN SPACE

Picture a slingshot. The rock that took down the giant Goliath received an energy boost when David pulled the sling way back. When the boy let go, the rock was propelled forward with added force, and moved far faster than if simply thrown. In the case of spaceflight, the spacecraft is the rock and the planet's gravitational field is the sling-shot. The bigger the planet, the greater its gravity—and the greater its ability to "assist" in increasing an object's speed as it flies by.

Michael Minovitch showed that gravity assist could reduce the time and fuel it would take for a spacecraft to travel from one planet to another. A gravity "slingshot" could give a boost to a spacecraft carrying heavy scientific equipment on a long journey to several planets.

It was this slingshot idea that helped make the dream of inter-planetary travel a reality.

ROCKET MAN

Gary Flandro realized that Michael's slingshot could propel a space-craft to all of the outer planets if they were in just the right place. So he looked at the sky maps, crunched some numbers, and drew some graphs. Eureka! A rare planetary alignment would occur during the 1980s. All the outer planets would be located on the same side of the solar system. They would be in the perfect arrangement for gravity assist. This would not happen again for another 176 years!

Gary did more math. He calculated that twenty years of travel time could be deducted from a trip to Neptune or Pluto using gravity assists. He proposed sending one spacecraft to fly by Jupiter, Saturn, Uranus, and Neptune, and a second craft to fly by Jupiter, Saturn, and Pluto. Gary named his idea the Grand Tour, and announced that the best time to launch was during the fall of 1977.

But some NASA scientists did not share Gary's excitement for the Grand Tour. They pointed out the negatives: *We've never built a space-craft that has operated for ten years! We want to build an expensive space telescope. We're also building a space shuttle. Sending robots to the planets will cost about $900 million. It's unaffordable.*

Gary's Grand Tour needed approval from NASA and President Richard Nixon. But Gary was only a student. He worked part-time at JPL. Gary had no say in anything. The Grand Tour was not approved. It was too expensive, too grandiose, and too far-flung.

But maybe a shorter mission to Jupiter and Saturn would fly. If it did, perhaps scientists could figure out a way to keep the Grand Tour option alive.

The Grand Tour would require a gravity assist from Jupiter to "slingshot" the spacecraft to Saturn. (Artist's rendering.)

65,000 PARTS AND 10,000 PATHS

In 1972 the cheaper and less ambitious Mariner Jupiter Saturn '77 (MJS-77) mission was approved. JPL had $250 million and five years to build two identical spacecraft. Why two? Not because twins are cute, but because stuff happens, and it's smart to have a backup plan. If spacecraft 1 "died" before getting to Saturn, for example, then spacecraft 2 would provide a second chance.

Thousands of people got busy. Physicists, astronomers, and chemists. Mechanical, thermal, software, and electrical engineers. Welders, electricians, machinists, seamsters, and wire wrappers. They worked in labs around the country—and the world—to design the mission and build each spacecraft's sixty-five thousand parts.

One of the engineers working on MJS-77 was navigation expert Charley Kohlhase. His job was to figure out the best flight paths to Jupiter out of ten thousand possibilities. Back in the early 1970s there wasn't much computing power, so Charley's team of twelve had to invent new software that could quickly design and simulate thousands of missions. They came up with two routes designed to take two spacecraft to Jupiter and Saturn. One spacecraft would fly close to Jupiter's large moon Io (EYE-oh). The other would focus on Saturn's big moon Titan. Together, the spacecraft would have close encounters with five of Jupiter's moons. Neither spacecraft would stop or land anywhere. Instead, they would zoom past, snapping pictures and collecting data on the fly.

One of those routes had already been mapped by Michael Minovitch ten years earlier. Using gravity assist, the spacecraft would slingshot from Jupiter to Saturn—and from there? Onward to Uranus, and maybe even Neptune. Charley kept the Grand Tour option alive with every move he made.

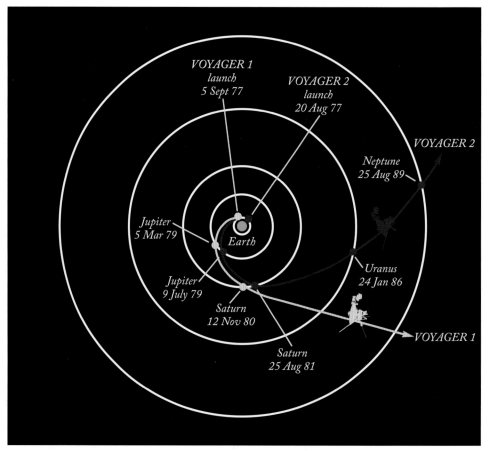

The proposed flight paths for the Voyagers. The massive gravity of the outer planets would increase the spacecraft's speed and propel them onward.

In 1977, a few months before launch, MJS-77 was renamed. John Casani, the mission project manager, said, "Who the hell cares about what year we launched the mission? We need a nice, crisp name." So the scientists held a contest. The prize for the winning name—Voyager—was a case of champagne.

THE JUNK ON THE BUS

Each Voyager weighed in at about 1,600 pounds (726 kilograms)—the same size and weight as a Volkswagen Rabbit (a peppy, fuel-efficient car back then). Each was built around a "bus," a ten-sided box containing ten compartments to house and protect science experiments, radio transmitters, and computers from radiation, dust, ice, and extreme cold. Every part and processor was state-of-the-art—the latest and greatest technology.

Today you need look no further than your grandmother's purse to find a more powerful computer than the ones on the Voyagers. The key fob to her Buick (or whatever she drives) is more powerful, her tablet is at least a million times faster, and her cell phone has more than 270,000 times as much memory. In fact, the technology on board the Voyagers is similar to the junk you might find down in your grandmother's basement.

Before iTunes, MP3 players, CD drives, and cassette tape players, there was the eight-track tape player. When the tape reached the end, it was rewound and played again, over and over—until the player "ate" it. Despite the inevitable tangled mess of tape, the eight-track was a huge leap in technology because it could be installed in a car.

Before the eight-track the only way to play an album was on a record player that spun a vinyl disk. A record player required a still and stable surface for the needle to maintain constant contact with the disk—difficult to do in a moving vehicle. The eight-track made it possible to crank favorite tunes on road trips without relying on the taste of the DJ at the local radio station.

Each Voyager had an eight-track player-recorder that was even more advanced. It could record scientific data in many forms, including images taken by the spacecraft's two TV cameras. The player-recorder had enough memory to store about one hundred pictures at a time. This storage capacity would come in handy while flying behind a moon or a planet, where the radio connection to Earth was blocked.

Later, when the spacecraft was back in contact, the pictures would be sent to Earth using the high-gain antenna installed on top of the bus.

BLASTOFF

Voyager 2 blasted into space on August 20, 1977. Sixteen days later, on September 5, Voyager 1 was launched on a trajectory designed to pass Voyager 2 in the asteroid belt. But as the rocket carrying Voyager 1 barreled through Earth's atmosphere, scientists realized something was wrong.

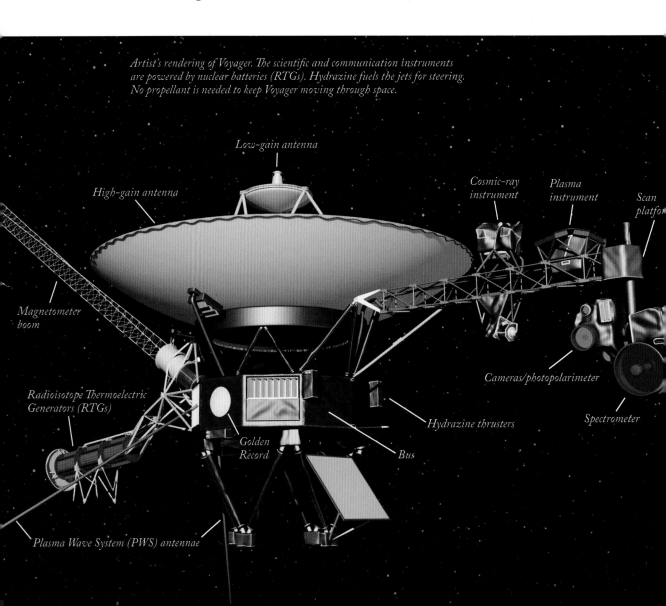

Artist's rendering of Voyager. The scientific and communication instruments are powered by nuclear batteries (RTGs). Hydrazine fuels the jets for steering. No propellant is needed to keep Voyager moving through space.

Low-gain antenna

Cosmic-ray instrument

Plasma instrument

Scan platfo

High-gain antenna

Magnetometer boom

Cameras/photopolarimeter

Radioisotope Thermoelectric Generators (RTGs)

Hydrazine thrusters

Spectrometer

Golden Record

Bus

Plasma Wave System (PWS) antennae

As Charley Kohlhase monitored the rocket's speed, he turned to his boss, Voyager project manager John Casani. "John," he said, "we may not be making it. We're not getting enough velocity."

The rocket was burning way too much fuel. Would it run out before reaching space? But then, with only 3.5 seconds of fuel left, Voyager 1 broke free of Earth's gravity and made it into orbit around the planet.

The cosmic cruise could commence.

TENACIOUS TWINS

Today, after forty years of continuous operation, the eight-track player-recorders aboard the Voyagers are still working. Although they are no longer recording pictures, they are collecting other data that is painting a brand-new picture of outer space.

Like Thing 1 and Thing 2, the mess makers in Dr. Seuss's *The Cat in the Hat*, Voyager 1 and Voyager 2 are tireless twins. They are literally "things." Yet they embody the human spirit. Built into their computer software is the capacity for change. Over the decades, they have been updated and reprogrammed, allowing them to adapt to their surroundings and extend their mission beyond the planets.

But hold on, let's not get ahead of them just yet! First we must meet the King.

KING JUPITER

It is the evening of January 7, 1610, and an Italian math teacher is looking through his handmade telescope. He spots Jupiter and then notices three bright stars never before seen, two to the east of the planet, one to the west. Night turns to morning and back to night. The professor looks through his telescope again. There is Jupiter, big and bright as ever, but the three little stars have moved. Now they are all to the west of the planet, lined up like ducks in a row! How is this possible? Stars don't change positions. The professor is excited. He returns to his telescope the next evening, but it's cloudy and he sees nothing. *Mamma mia!* He can hardly wait for nightfall the next day.

Jupiter's moons as observed by Galileo on January 7 and 8, 1610.

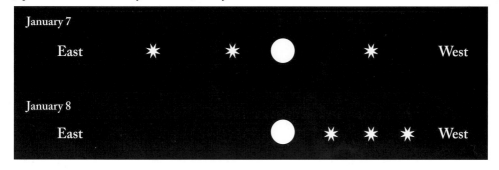

Opposite: Collage of Voyager 1 images showing Jupiter and its four large moons: Io (upper left), Europa (center), Ganymede (lower left), and Callisto (lower right). (Not to scale.)

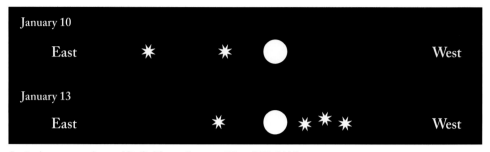

Jupiter's moons as observed by Galileo on January 10 and 13, 1610.

Finally, it is dark again and the sky is clear. There is Jupiter, but the stars are no longer lined up in the west. Tonight they are east of Jupiter, and there are only two of them. What's going on?

STARRY MESSENGERS

On January 13 Galileo Galilei looked through his telescope and for the first time ever saw four "starlets." He'd already determined that the stars wandering about Jupiter were not actually stars, but moons. Less than two months later, he published his discovery in his best seller, *The Starry Messenger.* The announcement was "earth-shattering" because it stated that other planets had their own orbiting moons—more evidence that Earth was not the center of the universe.

In 1632 Galileo was arrested by the Roman Catholic Church and locked up for the rest of his life. His crime? Refusing to take back his statement that Earth and the other planets revolve around the Sun.

Ten years later Galileo died, but the scientific revolution he ignited did not. Within months of Galileo's death, a tiny, sickly baby was born in England. His mother named him Isaac and abandoned him to his grandmother. Isaac grew up to become Sir Isaac Newton, the master-mind who explained exactly how objects move by fusing the ideas of Galileo and Johannes Kepler, the astronomer who had mapped the orbits of the planets around the Sun in 1609.

In 1665 English astronomer Robert Hooke and Italian astronomer Giovanni Cassini independently looked through their telescopes and discovered Jupiter's "Great Red Spot." Three hundred years later the NASA spacecraft Pioneer 10 got within 81,000 miles (130,357 kilometers) of Jupiter's cloud tops and discovered that the radiation around Jupiter was a million times stronger than that around Earth—five hundred times the deadly dose. Key information for designing spacecraft for a close encounter with the "gas giant."

CRUISE CONTROL

More than three centuries of scientific discovery paved the way for the Voyagers. After escaping Earth's gravity, the spacecraft set cruise control at 35,000 miles per hour (15.6 kilometers per second) and sped out to the asteroid belt located between Mars and Jupiter.

Few and far between, the asteroids did not pose much threat, but scientists back on Earth kept close watch and made mini course corrections to stay on track. On December 19, 1977, after only one week inside the asteroid belt, Voyager 1 passed its twin. The Voyagers cruised for another year, ready for the next stage of their mission: observation.

BIG AND LITTLE SCIENCE

Observation using the onboard scientific instruments was the whole point of the mission. The scientist in charge was Ed Stone, a physicist from Caltech. As the project scientist, Ed was the "decider."

"It turns out, that's a much more critical role than I had thought ahead of time," Ed later said. "By deciding to make this observation rather than that one, you're effectively deciding that that group of scientists gets to make a discovery and this group doesn't."

Voyager project scientist Ed Stone in 2013.

Ed had to manage eleven science teams, each with their own instruments aboard the Voyagers. This was "big science." "Big" because building the instruments and running the mission required thousands of people and millions of dollars—in one word, NASA. But it was also "little science." "Little" because individual scientists working in small labs around the country were doing the research and making the discoveries. Ed was the guy who made big science and little science work together. He believed that all the Voyager data should be shared as a group (big science), not owned by one scientist (little science). The way to do this, Ed decided, was to hold a press conference.

"I realized," explained Ed, "that with Voyager we had both the opportunity and the obligation to communicate what we were discovering. To help the media tell the story."

In other words, "show and tell."

During the press conference, graphics would do the showing. As the images and data streamed in from Voyager 1, artists would work all night, creating charts, graphs, and drawings that simplified difficult science for the public. Early the next morning the scientists would approve the graphics, then go on TV to tell their story.

As Voyager 1 sped toward Jupiter, all the science teams went into overdrive preparing for the encounter, each hoping for a great story that would make the news. But no one, not even Ed, could have imagined the stories the Voyagers would reveal.

FACE-TO-FACE WITH THE GIANT

The weather is always bad on Jupiter. Swirling hurricanes, speeding jet streams, 200-mile-per-hour (322 kilometer-per-hour) trade winds, lightning bolts, and toxic clouds form a thin skin around the planet.

Jupiter's Great Red Spot, a raging storm more than three times the size of Earth, photographed by Voyager 1.

As Voyager 1 approached this dangerous world, its camera went to work, taking one picture every two hours, then increasing photography to one shot every ninety-six seconds. Close-ups of the Great Red Spot showed a massive and complicated storm system composed of smaller storms. And as Jupiter's moons came into focus, scientists were stunned to find out that most of their predictions were dead wrong. The moons of Jupiter were not at all like Earth's. Instead, each was a unique world. Indeed, Jupiter was more than a mere planet. Like another Sun, it had a multitude of orbiting "planets" all its own.

LAVA LINDA

On Monday, March 5, 1979, Voyager 1 made its closest approach to Jupiter, flying within 128,400 miles (206,700 kilometers) of the planet. Researchers back on Earth eagerly awaited each "postcard" that streamed across space. One of those researchers, Linda Morabito, was an engineer at JPL, responsible for processing Voyager photographs.

By the time Friday night rolled around, Linda was extremely tired. She'd been working nonstop for weeks studying pictures. The newest shots were from 2.6 million miles (4.5 million kilometers) beyond Jupiter, looking back. By the time Linda saw the pictures, the spacecraft was long past Jupiter and on its way to Saturn.

Despite her exhaustion, Linda studied a picture of Jupiter's large moon Io. "What's that?" she asked herself out loud. A bulge jutting from the side of the crescent-shaped moon caught her eye. At first she wondered if it could be another moon. But Linda knew a moon that large would already have been discovered. The bulge looked more like a solar flare than anything else. But that was impossible.

Linda was doing "little science," just as she had done day in and day out for years. But as she looked at the picture of Io, she knew it

Voyager 1 image of Io, showing a gas plume from active volcano Loki. Linda Morabito was studying the inset image when she discovered the first evidence of extraterrestrial volcanic eruption.

would take "big science" to determine exactly what she had discovered. Over the weekend, teams of JPL scientists went to work analyzing the photographs of Io. On Monday morning Linda's phone rang. The call was from her colleague Peter Kupferman. He was upstairs.

"You'd better get up here!" he shouted. "They've found volcanoes all over the place! Everybody's gone crazy!"

Linda's "flare" was actually a plume of gas exploding out of a huge volcano. Never before had volcanoes been observed anywhere but on Earth. It turns out that Io is the most volcanic place in the solar system, spewing lava 190 miles (300 kilometers) into space at speeds of more than 2,200 miles per hour (1 kilometer per second).

RAVE NEW WORLDS

As Voyager 1 sped away from Jupiter, Voyager 2 was fast approaching. Jupiter's off-the-charts radiation had damaged the computers on Voyager 1, resulting in data loss and blurry photos. To avoid similar problems with Voyager 2, scientists uploaded new software to better position and protect the spacecraft from radiation damage. The fix worked, and Voyager 2 sent stunning images of Jupiter's moons to scientists waiting in suspense back on Earth.

Ganymede is huge. It is the biggest moon in the solar system, bigger than Mercury and almost as large as Mars. Voyager photos of Ganymede revealed impact craters, ruts, and grooves. Parts of Ganymede are as old as Jupiter—4.5 billion years—but there's also newer icy terrain.

Europa looked icy smooth and impossibly flat. Scientists wondered what lay beneath that glassy glacial surface. Perhaps an ocean of liquid water? If so, then possibly life existed under the ice. There was no way to know for sure, but the Voyager pictures would inspire future missions.

Pictures of Callisto showed an icy surface marred with scars and craters from billions of years of impacts. Without lava flows or active glaciers to remake its surface, there are more craters on Callisto than on any other place in the solar system.

But why? Why does Callisto lack the internal heat that creates volcanoes on Io and likely melts ice into water on Europa and Ganymede? One of the answers may involve orbital resonance. Picture orbital resonance as a circle dance. Every time the dancer on the outside (Ganymede) completes one full circle around Jupiter, the middle dancer (Europa) goes around twice, and the inner dancer (Io) makes four full circles. Sometimes the dancers pass each other at exactly the same time. When this happens the moons pull on each other, changing the shape of their orbits. Sometimes the moons are pulled closer to Jupiter; at other times they are pulled away. The changing gravitational force creates "tides" inside the moon—similar to the tides on Earth created by our moon's gravitational pull. The tidal movement creates friction, resulting in heat that melts rock into lava and ice into water.

But Callisto is Jupiter's outermost moon and is not part of the dance. It does not experience orbital resonance. The result is an isolated world frozen in time.

RINGS AROUND THE ROSIE

Galileo would have been blown away by Voyager's images of Jupiter's moons. Ed Stone and his scientific team were bowled over when Voyager 1 discovered that Jupiter has more than one ring. "There's one lesson we learned from Voyager," said Ed. "Nature is much more inventive than our imaginations."

Scientists determined that Jupiter's rings are made of microscopic rocks and dust that are constantly lost and replaced by Jupiter's four inner moons. Only one of these moons, Amalthea, was known before Voyager 1 found Thebe and Metis, and Voyager 2 revealed Adrastea.

ON THE ROAD AGAIN

By the end of August 1979, Voyager 2 had taken more than thirty-three thousand photos at Jupiter, adding to Voyager 1's nineteen thousand postcards. A brand-new picture of the solar system was emerging, and this was only the beginning.

It took twenty months for Voyager 1 to drive out to Saturn, thirty months for Voyager 2. Scientists used the time to fine-tune the trajectories for the best possible encounters with that planet's rings and moons. In October 1980 Voyager 1 approached Saturn, the next gas giant, revealing a drama of epic proportions.

LORD OF THE RINGS

TRACK

4

The year is 1855, and twenty-four-year-old James Clerk Maxwell is trying to win a contest. Can he figure out the "Saturn Problem," a mystery that has perplexed astronomers for two hundred years?

Back in 1610 Galileo became the first person to see Saturn's rings, but he had no idea what they were. Maybe they were the planet's ears, he joked. In 1659 Dutch scientist Christiaan Huygens published an article describing his observations of a ring around Saturn. And in 1675 French astronomer Jean-Dominique Cassini observed that Saturn's ring was actually two rings. He named the darker outer ring "A" and the inner, brighter one "B." In 1850 a third ring even closer to Saturn was discovered and named "C." But no one knew how or why the rings formed.

Were the rings liquid? Did they flow in streams around the planet? Or were they solid pieces of something, and if so, how did they orbit without breaking apart? Maybe they were just smithereens, moving together in an organized pattern. For two centuries, the Saturn Problem defeated many brilliant minds.

False-color view of Saturn's rings created by computer processing of an image taken by Voyager 2.

Enter James, a guy who likes a challenge. If he can solve the Saturn Problem, he'll win the prestigious Adams Prize and the hefty sum of 130 British pounds. James can use the money. But more important, James is fascinated by the physical world. He wants to know everything that is possible to know. James is determined to win.

First he proves that the rings cannot be a solid structure. By combining math equations in new ways, he shows that a solid ring is possible only if it is extremely lopsided. But Saturn's rings are not lopsided.

James does some more calculations and proves that the rings cannot exist as fluids. If they were liquid, they would break up into blobs and no longer look like rings. By the process of elimination, James concludes that Saturn's rings are made of many pieces of solid matter. But the rules of the contest say he must prove it mathematically, so James does more computations involving vibrations, density, ratios, and friction. He wins the prize.

Voyager 1 took this photo of Saturn and its moons Tethys (top) and Dione.

REMEMBER THE TITAN

When the Voyagers finally made it to Saturn, they confirmed everything James Maxwell predicted about the rings—and more. First, Voyager 1 flew within 4,000 miles (6,400 kilometers) of Titan, Saturn's largest moon. Scientists hoped a close encounter with the moon might help answer the burning question: Is there life beyond Earth?

Astronomers knew from telescopic studies that Titan's atmosphere is similar to that of the ancient Earth, before living cells added oxygen. In 1979, data gathered by Pioneer 11 showed that the moon is way too cold to support life as we know it. Voyager 1 confirmed that Titan is so cold that its rocks are actually ice—in a warmer climate they would be liquid or gas. The thick clouds around Titan are not made of water like clouds on Earth, but are methane, ethane, and other carbon-containing chemicals known as organic compounds. Carbon is the signature element of all living things. Could there be bizarre life-forms growing in the "toxic" rivers, lakes, and oceans of organic chemicals beneath Titan's clouds?

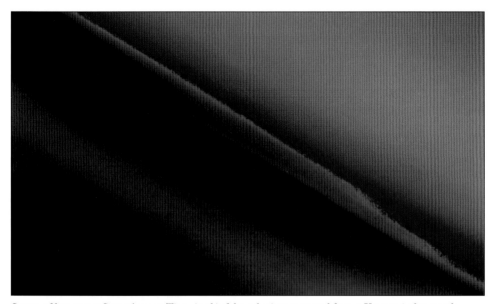

Layers of haze cover Saturn's moon Titan in this false-color image created from a Voyager 1 photograph.

Based on Voyagers' discoveries, scientists now agree that if life exists on Titan, it would truly be out of this world. Instead of requiring water, life-forms on Titan would depend on chemicals that flow at extremely cold temperatures.

RINGS AND THINGS

On November 12, 1980, Voyager 1 sped past Titan and through Saturn's orbiting rings. Radio signals revealed the rings are made from particles of pure water-ice ranging in size from tiny chips to blocks as big as a four-bedroom house. Photographs showed that the gaps between the rings are not empty space as previously imagined, but interwoven with braided twists and interconnected by strange, spoke-like structures—patterns that are still a mystery.

Voyager 1 discovered two "shepherd" moons, Pandora and Prometheus, orbiting outside the F ring (discovered by Pioneer 11). Like shepherds herding sheep, they influence the movement of particles within the F ring.

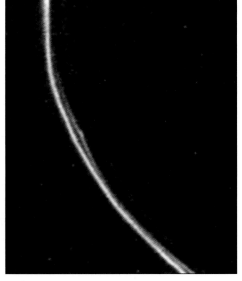

Left: Mysterious "spoke" features (dark splotches) in Saturn's B ring.
Right: Close-up view of "braided" strands in Saturn's F Ring

Cameras aboard the spacecraft shot still-life portraits of the planet and its moons and rings. They also tracked the movement of clouds using time-lapse photography. Saturn's winds blow at 1,100 miles per hour (500 meters per second) and are strongest at the equator. Saturn is cold: –312°F (–191°C) in its upper atmosphere, and even colder at the north pole. Its atmosphere is mostly hydrogen and helium—similar to Jupiter and the Sun—but Saturn has less helium than scientists expected.

In less than forty-eight hours, Voyager 1 completed its visit of Saturn. But because of its close encounter with Titan, rather than with Saturn itself, Voyager 1 did not slingshot to the next planet. Instead, it began its journey out of the solar system.

Voyager 1's successful encounter with Saturn paved the way for Voyager 2's ultra-close visit. On August 25, 1981, Voyager 2 streamed more spectacular photos. Scientists saw a single ring strand in the F ring "unraveling" and later coming back together again. Inside the "braid" were tiny moonlets about 10 miles (16 kilometers) across—much smaller than the larger "shepherd" moons found by Voyager 1. All together, the Voyagers discovered six small moons and another ring scientists named "G."

"Over and over, the spacecraft revealed so many unexpected things that it often took days, months and even years to figure them out," said Ed Stone thirty years after the Voyagers first saw the mysterious braid in the F ring.

As Voyager 2 passed through Saturn's rings, the planet's gravity boosted its speed from 36,000 to 54,000 miles per hour (16 to 24 kilometers per second). Scientists worried that the accelerating spacecraft might be impacted by a piece of ice or dust. A single ring particle smaller than a grain of sand could easily destroy the spacecraft.

Adding to the drama, Voyager 2 would soon disappear behind Saturn. (Both Voyagers flew behind every planet they visited as they were flung on to their next destination.) For ninety-five minutes, the spacecraft would be completely out of touch. Scientists preprogrammed the camera to photograph rings, clouds, storms, and moons—maybe even auroras and lightning bolts. Then, on the night of August 25, 1981, they waited.

GROUND CONTROL TO VOYAGER 2

At 10:26 p.m. Pasadena time, Voyager 2 disappeared behind Saturn and its feed stopped. Then, at one minute past midnight, it reappeared, all in one piece. The scientific community breathed a sigh of relief. But as the postcards streamed in, it became clear that something was very wrong.

Image team member Candice "Candy" Hansen had slept in the back of her pickup truck so she could be at the lab when the images started arriving. The first pictures recorded on the eight-track and beamed back to Earth were of Saturn's large moons, Enceladus and Tethys. The next shots were supposed to be edge-on views of the rings. But the screen was black. A few minutes later, a detailed shot of the A ring appeared, but Candy and her colleagues noticed that it wasn't the photo they had programmed.

"I wanted to cry," said Candy. "But I told myself that professionals don't sob in front of their colleagues. Then I got to work on figuring out what had happened and what we could do about it."

On Saturn's far side, the cameras aboard Voyager 2 had misbehaved. Aimed in odd directions, the cameras captured off-center shots showing rims of moons and slivers of rings. Had the spacecraft collided with a microscopic ice cube? Highly unlikely. It was still flying on target, straight on course. More likely, the camera-scan platform was moving too quickly, its gears requiring more lubricant than was available.

Within hours, engineers uploaded new commands to the onboard computers that controlled the camera-scan platform. The new software decreased the platform's speed and the number of movements it made. This slower, gentler approach was easier on the gears, but also resulted in fewer images and less data. Using remote-control commands, Candy and the other scientists pointed the cameras back at Saturn and snapped shot after shot of the shrinking ringed planet.

RAMBLE ON

Voyager 2's close encounter with Saturn flung it on toward Uranus. The distance was twice as far as the voyage from Jupiter to Saturn.

The long journey gave JPL engineers five years to figure out how to fix another problem with the cameras. In extremely low light, cameras compensate with long exposure times. But if the camera moves, the picture comes out blurry. On the Voyagers, whenever the recorder was turned on, the spacecraft jiggled a little. Out in deep, dark space, even the slightest movement produced blurry photos.

Back on Earth, the engineers tinkered with their test Voyager to figure out how to counteract the jiggling. They learned that by firing the thrusters at exactly the same time the recorder turned on, they could cancel out the movement. They then taught Voyager 2 new dance steps by reprogramming the entire spacecraft to move in graceful ways that would prevent blurry photos and missed shots.

Late in 1985 Voyager 2 was ready for the first and only encounter with the icy blue-green giant Uranus, named for the father of Saturn, the husband of Gaia (Earth), and the god of the sky.

TOTALLY TILTED

Although he doesn't know it yet, tonight is the night of William Herschel's life. It's March 13, 1781, and William is looking through his homemade telescope when he sees a "curious either nebulous star or perhaps a comet." He records his observation in a notebook.

This is the week of his younger sister Caroline's thirty-first birthday. It's also the week they're moving across Bath, their adopted home in England. Usually Caroline is at William's side, writing down observations, but not during this busy week.

When Caroline returns on March 23, she takes over the notebook and records the comet's movements, night after night. But William and Caroline are starting to wonder if the comet is really a comet. Where is its tail? And why does it move along a circular arc? Comets follow a U-shaped curve. During the summer the comet disappears from view, but it returns in August, still showing none of the characteristics of a true comet.

Voyager 2 studied Uranus for 5.5 hours on January 24, 1986. A blue haze hid the cloud details from view.

In November 1781 the Herschels, along with dozens of astronomers worldwide, agree that the comet is actually a planet. This is a first. No one has ever "discovered" a planet before. All the other planets have been known since ancient times, seen with the naked eye as specks of light wandering the zodiac.

MIDSUMMER NIGHT'S DREAM

More than two hundred years after William and Caroline observed their mysterious new planet, Voyager 2 sped by Uranus at 51,000 miles per hour (22.8 kilometers per second). It was midsummer on the planet's south pole, where Voyager 2 would make its closest encounter from 50,679 miles (81,500 kilometers) out. Like an arrow hurtling on a bull's-eye trajectory, Voyager 2 threaded its way through multiple moons and behind the planet, analyzing the atmosphere and gaining

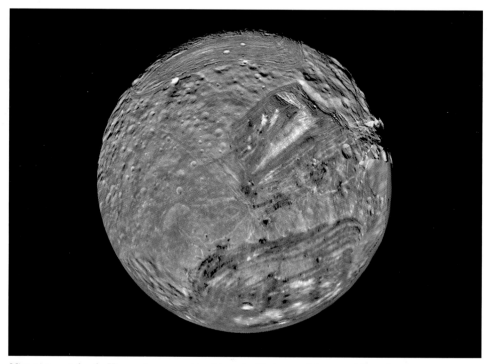

Nine pictures taken by Voyager 2 were combined to make this image of the moon Miranda.

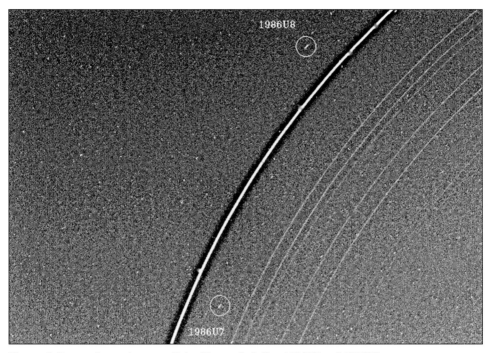

Voyager 2 discovered several moons orbiting Uranus, including 1986U7 and 1986U8.

maximum gravity assist for the trip out to Neptune. As a result, the only moon the spacecraft came close to was Miranda.

Up close and personal, Miranda was a small world of rock and ice only 300 miles (500 kilometers) across. With towering ice cliffs 10 miles (16 kilometers) high, deep gouges and grooves some twelve times deeper than the Grand Canyon, and a jumbled patchwork of scrapes and scars, Miranda was revealed as one of the strangest places in the solar system. Scientists wondered if it was shattered to pieces, then put back together again. But recent research now suggests that melting ice pushing from inside caused the twisted terrain.

Ten hours later, Uranus was in Voyager's "rearview mirror." Voyager had discovered ten new moons, and with the camera pointed back at the Sun, it snapped photos of eleven rings orbiting the planet—two more than previously known.

A DIFFERENT SPIN

Discovering new moons and rings in the solar system was by now practically old hat for Voyager. But Uranus was unique.

"We knew Uranus would be different because it's tipped on its side," explained Ed Stone. "We expected surprises."

One of the scientists studying Uranus was Heidi Hammel, a graduate student at the University of Hawai'i. Later Heidi spoke about her research: "Something strange must have happened to Uranus," she said. It was "just personally so screwed up."

How could a planet be screwed up? What was Heidi talking about?

Most planets spin like tops as they orbit the Sun. But Uranus spins on its side. It's totally tilted.

Summer on Uranus lasts for twenty years at the lit pole. The Sun shines constantly—there is no night. At the dark pole, on the opposite side of the planet, it is winter and always night. During spring and

Uranus rotates sideways on its axis, rolling around the Sun every 84 Earth years. Summer is about 20 years of nonstop sunshine, while winter is 20 years of total darkness.

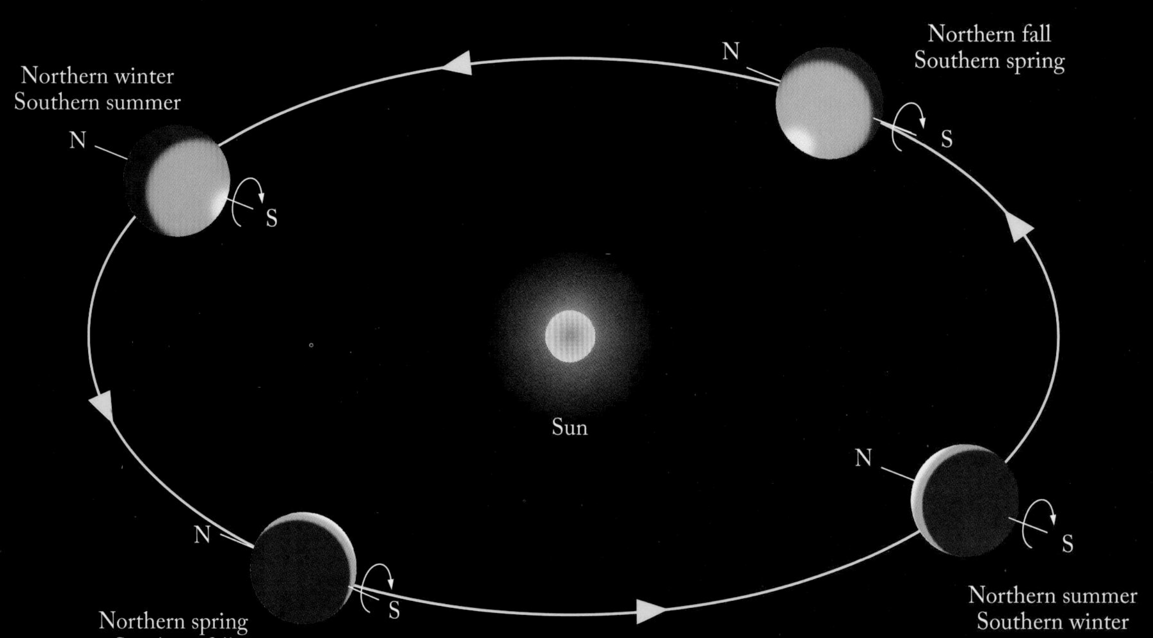

Northern fall
Southern spring

N

S

Northern winter
Southern summer

N

S

Sun

N

S

Northern summer
Southern winter

N

S

Northern spring

fall the Sun shines on the planet's equator. But because the equator is vertical with respect to the orbit, the entire planet has dark nights and sunny days—every day for twenty years. Despite these radically changing seasons, the temperature on Uranus is always about −350°F (−212°C).

ICY GIANT

Like Jupiter and Saturn, Uranus is a gas giant. Its atmosphere is mostly hydrogen and helium, although it also contains methane, which gives it its blue-green color.

Deep beneath its cloud tops, however, Uranus is radically different from Jupiter and Saturn. It does not have a dense hydrogen interior, where huge pressure turns hydrogen gas into hot, swirling liquid metal. Instead, inside Uranus, there's an "icy" slurry of chemicals— solid(-ish) water, ammonia, and methane. Think "toxic blue Slushie."

Scientists define ice on Earth as a substance that freezes at cold temperatures. Water, of course, is one. Ammonia and methane are, as well. But the ice inside Uranus is different from ice on Earth because it's formed not by low temperature, but by extreme pressure. That pressure forces the water, ammonia, and methane into a dense mixture that resembles slush. This ice exists even at temperatures above the freezing point. Because Uranus is mostly composed of ice, it is classified as an ice giant (a type of gas giant).

At its core, Uranus is 8,540°F (4,727°C). Although this sounds hot, it's frigid compared to the core temperature of Jupiter, which is more than six times hotter. Everything is relative!

Even with its hot, dense ocean of chemicals deep inside, the surface temperature of Uranus is much colder than expected. Why?

Nobody knows.

This false-color, high-contrast image of Uranus highlights subtle differences in the atmosphere at the planet's south pole. Scientists think there may be a cap of haze or smog over the pole, represented here in green.

SPACE ODDITY

There's a lot of weirdness out at Uranus. Its extremely low surface temperature and total tilt are odd, for sure, but it also has a bizarrely shaped magnetic field. Before Voyager 2, scientists weren't sure if Uranus even had a magnetic field. Earth, Mercury, Saturn, and Jupiter have magnetic fields created by electric currents generated inside their melted cores. These fields take the same shape as iron filings around a magnet.

If iron filings could be sprinkled around Uranus, the result would be twisted lines. Scientists do not know the source of Uranus's spiral magnetic field. But they confirm that a compass wouldn't work there.

Space oddity, indeed!

LET'S DANCE

Planets dance around the Sun. Moons and rings dance around the planets. And the Voyagers danced around them all, taking pictures, collecting data, and transforming how humans see and understand the solar system.

For the next three years, Voyager 2 cruised onward, eager to meet its last partner of the night, for one more planetary tango.

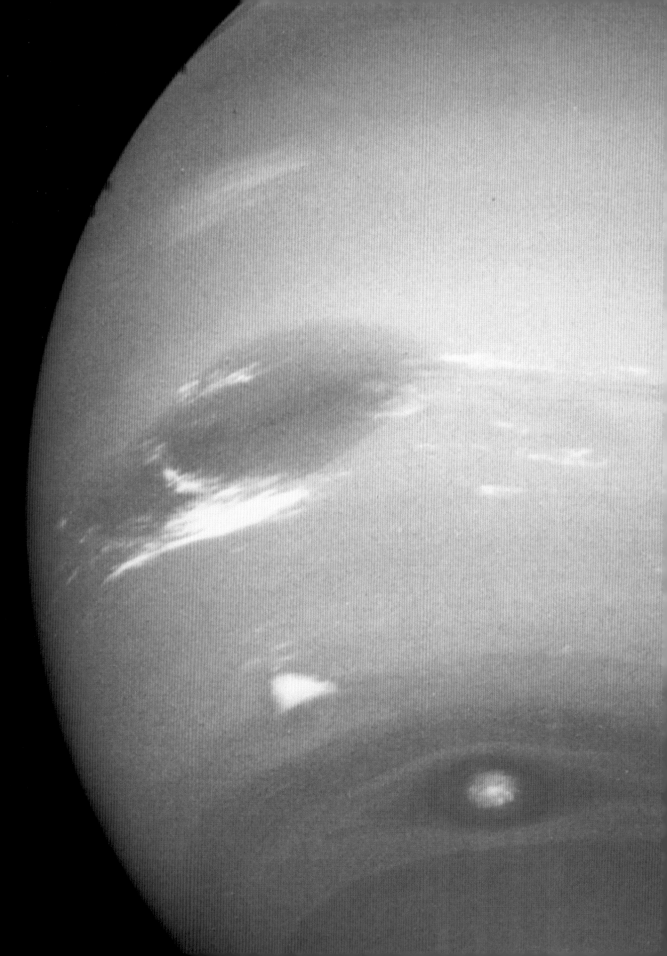

LAST TANGO IN SPACE

TRACK

6

Tonight is September 23, 1846, and Caroline Herschel is still alive. She's ninety-six years old. Although she doesn't know it yet, she has lived long enough to witness another amazing planetary event, even more spectacular than her brother's discovery of Uranus.

It's been sixty-five years since Caroline and William noticed that the orbit of Uranus was not what they expected based on Newton's theories of gravity. It appeared that something was pulling Uranus out of its predicted orbit, but Caroline and William had no idea what.

Eventually, after decades of observing the movement of Uranus, astronomers concluded that there must be another planet even farther away. What else could exert such a powerful force of gravity on Uranus? But finding such a distant planet through a telescope seemed impossible, because astronomers did not know where to look.

Until now.

This image of Neptune was created from two pictures taken by Voyager 2. The "Great Dark Spot" (top), "Scooter" (middle), and "Dark Spot 2" (bottom) are fast-moving storms and clouds.

Astronomer Johann Gottfried Galle of the Berlin Observatory in Germany knows exactly where to look. He's just received a letter containing the information. Not from a soothsayer or fortune-teller, but from a French mathematician named Urbain Le Verrier.

Johann points his telescope according to Urbain's instructions. There are many stars in view, but soon enough a miniature blue disk comes into focus. Midnight comes and goes as Johann observes the disk. Sunlight washes away the night. But Johann returns to his telescope the next night, and the next. As expected, the disk has moved from its original position. Johann is convinced—it is not a star, but a brand-new planet! He can hardly believe it, but he's seen it with his own eyes. He writes to Urbain, "The planet whose position you have described, really exists." The eighth planet has finally been discovered. And the mystery of Uranus's unpredictable path is solved!

BIG DEAL

The discovery of Neptune, named after the Roman god of the sea, was a big deal. Not only because its location expanded the solar system another billion miles (1.6 billion kilometers) deeper into space, but also because its existence was predicted using math. Newton's theories were now laws.

The discovery of Neptune was also a big controversy. Urbain Le Verrier was not the only mathematician who predicted its location. John Couch Adams of England conducted the same mathematical calculations and came to the same conclusion at least ten months earlier.

John also wrote a letter explaining the existence and location of the eighth planet. But his letter was addressed to the head of the Cambridge Observatory in England. Apparently the letter was ignored! To make up for this mix-up, the Adams Prize (recall the Saturn

Problem) was established by Cambridge University a few years later. Today, both John Couch Adams and Urbain Le Verrier are credited with the discovery of Neptune. And the Adams Prize is still one of the most prestigious mathematical science awards.

A few weeks after Neptune was first viewed through a telescope, its largest moon was discovered and named Triton, after one of the mythical Neptune's sons. Most moons are "in step" with their planet, orbiting in the same direction as the planet's orbit around the Sun. But astronomers figured out that Triton orbited Neptune backward— in the opposite direction from Neptune's motion. They knew little else about the far-flung moon.

In the summer of 1989, Voyager 2 was on its way to change that— and to exponentially expand our understanding of Triton, and everything else about Neptune.

STEPPIN' FAR OUT

Before arriving at Neptune, Voyager 2 learned a whole new set of high-tech dance steps. The Voyager team uploaded software that enabled the spacecraft to move into optimal positions to capture clear images in a cold, dark sky more than 2.8 billion miles (4.5 billion kilometers) from the Sun.

Neptune receives less than half of the light shining on Uranus, and only 3 percent of the light received by Jupiter. Since solar energy helps drive weather events, such as Jupiter's massive storms, some scientists predicted the weather on Neptune would be boring.

Candy Hansen and Heidi Hammel were among the first scientists to prove *that* weather forecast wrong. When Voyager 2 was still 60 million miles (97 million kilometers) away from Neptune, Candy and Heidi spotted a big dark spot on the planet's southern hemisphere.

When they did the math, they discovered that the spot was a storm the size of Earth. Eventually they determined that wind speeds on Neptune are the fastest in the solar system. At 1,500 miles per hour (671 meters per second), they're three times faster than the winds on Jupiter and nine times stronger than the most powerful hurricanes on Earth.

As Voyager 2 got closer and closer to Neptune, scientists saw that the "Great Dark Spot" was oval, not round like Jupiter's Great Red Spot. It also changed rapidly, with clouds coming and going.

Even though it receives far less sunlight than Uranus, Neptune is not as cold. The radical difference in temperature between Neptune's hot core, estimated to be 12,632°F (7,000°C), and its frigid surface, averaging –353°F (–214°C), creates extreme weather at the surface.

But where *is* the "surface" of a world where there is no solid ground on which to stand? On Neptune, clouds of frozen methane top a hydrogen-helium atmosphere. Below are clouds made of water and ammonia. Beneath the cloud layers there's a watery ocean of chemicals,

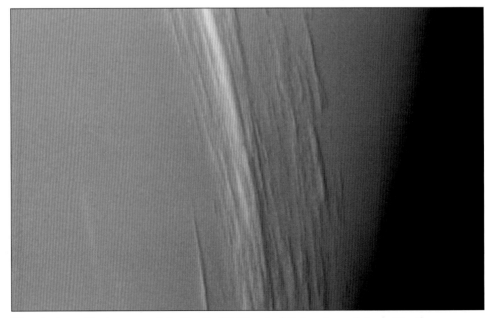

These clouds over Neptune appear to be 31 miles (50 kilometers) high and range between 31 miles (50 kilometers) and 124 miles (200 kilometers) wide.

This false-color photo of Neptune helped scientists measure the thickness of haze around the planet.

which becomes thicker and hotter with depth. Scientists define the surface of Neptune (and all the gas planets) as the place where the pressure is equal to Earth's air pressure at sea level (14.7 pounds per square inch or 101,353 pascals).

Of the four gas giants in our solar system, only two—Neptune and Uranus—are classified as ice giants. So far, Voyager has been the only mission to these ice giants, so scientists can only imagine what it's like inside these faraway worlds. Experiments on Earth show that methane can form diamonds when it is compressed under enormous pressure at ultrahigh temperatures. So diamond rain may fall on Neptune, and oceans of liquid diamond may exist deep within the planet. Deeper down, massive diamonds, swept under by ferocious surf, may sink and surface, creating a turbulent inner world capable of causing immense storms on the surface.

HELLO, GOODBYE

Early in the morning of August 25, 1989, Voyager 2 drove within 3,000 miles (4,950 kilometers) of Neptune's north pole. This was the closest it had come to any planet during its twelve-year journey.

A few hours later it sped within 25,000 miles (40,234 kilometers) of Triton, shooting pictures of its bright, icy surface. At −391°F (−235°C), Triton is the coldest place in the solar system. Voyager 2 also discovered that Triton has a thin atmosphere of nitrogen, methane, water, and carbon dioxide. The moon's surface is made of frozen nitrogen, making it look like a frosted globe. But the most amazing discovery was the plumes of nitrogen gas shooting five miles (eight kilometers) high. Like the volcanoes on Io, geysers on Triton were a total surprise.

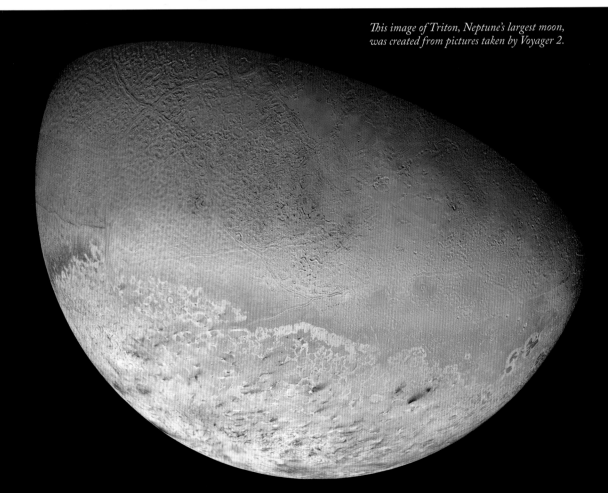

This image of Triton, Neptune's largest moon, was created from pictures taken by Voyager 2.

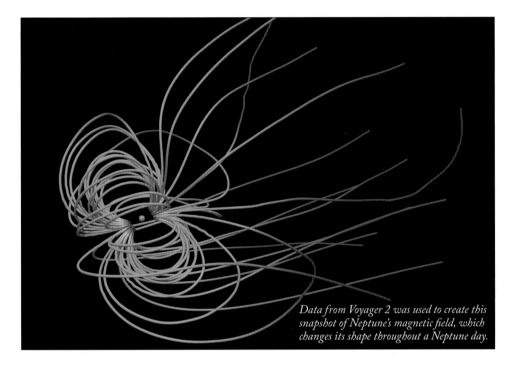

Data from Voyager 2 was used to create this snapshot of Neptune's magnetic field, which changes its shape throughout a Neptune day.

Voyager 2 also discovered that Neptune has a magnetic field twenty-seven times more powerful than Earth's. Like the magnetic field of Uranus, it's tilted—even though Neptune is not.

Before Voyager, astronomers weren't sure if Neptune had rings. All they could see from Earth were dark, disconnected arcs. But Voyager's postcards home revealed five dark rings. Voyager also discovered six new moons around the planet.

DANCING WITH THE STARS

Neptune's dance around the Sun takes 165 Earth years. Voyager 2's close-up dance with Neptune lasted less than six hours. It took four hours to receive pictures back on Earth, even though they were transmitted at the speed of light. By the time scientists saw the final snapshot of Neptune and Triton receding in the distance, the spacecraft was heading south toward the edge of the solar system, on its way to the stars.

COSMIC CRUISERS

TRACK

7

It is June 6, 1990, and Voyager 1's valentine from the edge of the solar system has finally been delivered. Despite being radioed at the speed of light, each pixel has taken five and a half hours to reach Earth, during nearly four months of intermittent transmission. The "Picture of the Century" is ready for framing.

SUSPENDED IN A SUNBEAM

Voyager image team expert Candy Hansen analyzed the images, just as she'd done since 1977. "I was all alone, actually, that afternoon, in my office," Candy later remembered. "I knew the data was coming back, and I wanted to see how it had turned out."

She found Neptune, a blurry blue bead in a sapphire-specked sea. There was Uranus, smeared like a drip of wet paint. She located Saturn, a golden halo. Crescent Mars was too dim to see, and tiny Mercury was so close to the Sun that it was obliterated in the glare. Venus was visible, less than a pixel of light. When Candy looked for Earth, all she saw were red, orange, and yellow sunbeams splashed across the black canvas of space. Where in the world was it?

One frame from the first-ever "portrait" of the solar system, taken by Voyager 1. Can you find Earth?

Finally Candy found Earth inside a yellow sunbeam.

"It was just a little dot, about two pixels big, three pixels big, so not very large," she said. "You know, I still get chills down my back because here was our planet, bathed in this ray of light, and it just looked incredibly special."

A PALE BLUE DOT

Voyager image-team scientist Carl Sagan had come up with the plan to shoot this special photo.

"The point of such a picture," he wrote, "would not be mainly scientific. . . . Our planet would be just a point of light. But I thought that—like the frame-filling Apollo photographs of the whole Earth—. . . it might be useful . . . as perspective on our place in the Cosmos."

When Carl saw the picture, he named it "Pale Blue Dot." The photograph shows Earth as a pinprick of light in an ocean of space. It's what a space traveler would see approaching the Sun from nearly 4 billion miles (6.4 billion kilometers) out.

It's also the last photograph the Voyagers will ever take. To save power, the cameras aboard the Voyagers have been shut down since 1990. But the spacecraft are still sending back a "picture" of outer space. This picture can't be seen with eyes. Instead, it is data about invisible things like ultraviolet rays, cosmic particles, plasma waves, and magnetic fields—measurements collected by sensors aboard the spacecraft. As they analyze this data, scientists are making new discoveries about the outer reaches of our solar system—and beyond.

HERE COMES THE SUN

Interstellar space is the space between the stars. It begins where "Sun space" ends.

The Sun is a star. At its core is a powerhouse where hydrogen fuses under billions of pounds of pressure to create helium. This nuclear reaction releases a huge amount of energy.

It takes millions of years for the energy released inside the core to radiate into the Sun's outer atmosphere, or corona. The corona is more than 1.8 million °F (1 million °C), which is even hotter than its surface. At this extreme temperature, the Sun's gravity is unable to keep the corona from blowing away in all directions at speeds of about 900,000

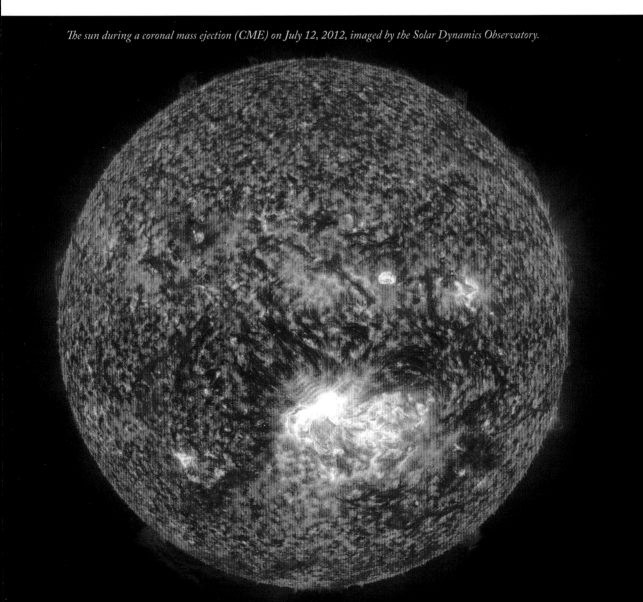

The sun during a coronal mass ejection (CME) on July 12, 2012, imaged by the Solar Dynamics Observatory.

miles per hour (400 kilometers per second). This streaming outward of the Sun's atmosphere is the solar wind.

Similar to the winds on Earth, the solar wind blows, gusts, and is calm, depending on the weather. Weather in the solar system, whether on Earth or in space, is created by uneven solar heating. But the solar wind differs from wind on Earth because it is made of plasma, which scientists define as the fourth state of matter. The first three states, solids, liquids, and gases, exist on Earth. But most of the matter scientists can observe in the universe exists as plasma.

Plasma is formed when atoms of gas in a star's corona become so hot that they are ripped apart. These positive and negative charged particles are the plasma that blows across space.

BURSTING OUR BUBBLE

Interstellar space is dominated by interstellar wind—plasma gusting from other stars—and atoms created in the Big Bang, when the universe first began. Sun space, or the heliosphere, is dominated by the solar wind—plasma spewed from the Sun. Picture the heliosphere as a long soap bubble made by waving a wand in the wind.

Inside the heliosphere bubble, the solar wind zips relentlessly outward. But as the solar wind blows farther and farther away from the Sun, it reaches the termination shock, the place where it collides with the interstellar wind and suddenly slows down. Beyond the termination shock is the heliosheath, literally the "skin of the Sun": it is the boundary between Sun space and star space. At the edge of the heliosheath, billions of miles from the Sun, the solar wind ceases. This is the heliopause.

Where does the heliosphere end and interstellar space begin? Only the Voyagers can tell us when they have burst through the bubble.

GUIDE TO THE GALAXY

Before Voyager, scientists had theories about the outer regions of the heliosphere, but no data. They imagined the termination shock as a fixed boundary, like the goal line on a football field. They pictured the heliopause as a place in space where our solar system ends and interstellar space begins.

As the Voyagers sped on, scientists got a clearer and clearer picture of space. For more than a decade, the spacecraft approached the termination shock. When they finally got there, they discovered a flexible

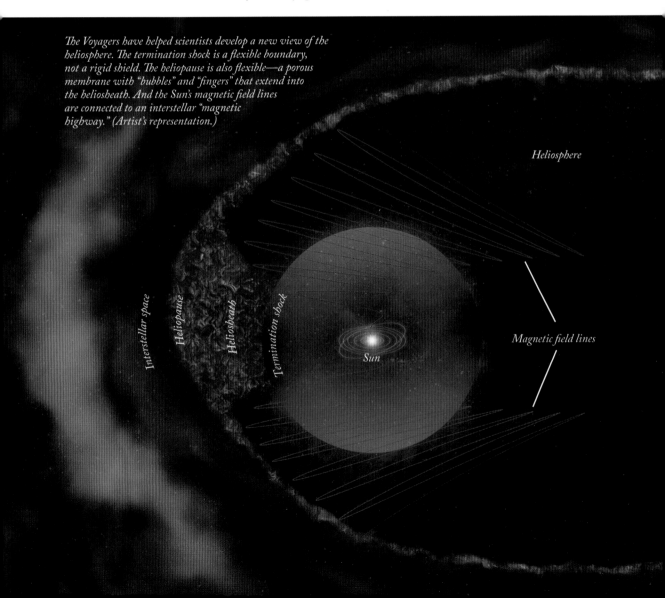

The Voyagers have helped scientists develop a new view of the heliosphere. The termination shock is a flexible boundary, not a rigid shield. The heliopause is also flexible—a porous membrane with "bubbles" and "fingers" that extend into the heliosheath. And the Sun's magnetic field lines are connected to an interstellar "magnetic highway." (Artist's representation.)

Heliosphere

Interstellar space

Heliopause

Heliosheath

Termination shock

Sun

Magnetic field lines

boundary, which they crossed and recrossed several times over a two-day period.

"No one has been to interstellar space before, and it's like traveling with guidebooks that are incomplete," said Ed Stone. "Still, uncertainty is part of exploration. We wouldn't go exploring if we knew exactly what we'd find."

CATCH A WAVE

The Plasma Science Experiment (PLS) aboard the Voyagers was designed to measure plasma from the Sun and other stars—and to detect the exact moment the spacecraft entered interstellar space. But in 1980, Voyager 1's PLS broke. Still, scientists had other ways to observe the spacecraft's surroundings.

The heliosphere bubble surrounding the Sun extends into space, contracting and expanding depending on what is happening on the Sun. Sometimes a magnetic cloud of plasma explodes out of the Sun. This coronal mass ejection (CME) creates a "tsunami wave" of pressure—a shock wave that vibrates ahead of it across space.

"Normally, interstellar space is like a quiet lake," explains Ed. "But when our sun has a burst, it sends a shock wave outward that reaches Voyager about a year later."

When the wave collides with the denser plasma in interstellar space, it "shocks" the plasma—or "excites" it, as scientists say. The energy of the interstellar plasma temporarily changes, and that change can be detected with another instrument, called the Plasma Wave System (PWS).

In March 2012 a large CME created a shock wave that moved into interstellar space. The wave excited the plasma surrounding Voyager 1, enabling the PWS to "listen" to the wave speeding past. As Ed

Stone put it, the wave caused the plasma "to resonate—'sing' or vibrate like a bell."

The PWS doesn't actually hear sound. Instead, it senses changes that can be measured in hertz (Hz), the same units used to measure sound. When the data from Voyager 1's PWS was played through a loudspeaker, the pitch changed from a low of 300 Hz to a high of 3,000 Hz. (On Earth a middle C on the piano is 261.6 Hz and the highest key is over 4,000 Hz.) When scientists heard the pitch change from low to high, they could tell that Voyager 1 was indeed outside the heliosphere—surrounded by the plasma of interstellar space.

BREAK ON THROUGH (TO THE OTHER SIDE)

Even though the PWS confirmed that Voyager 1 had entered interstellar space, other data showed that it was still inside the Sun's magnetic field. How was it possible that the magnetic field of the Sun could extend into interstellar space?

To answer the question, Ed Stone called his science teams together. It took three long meetings over the course of a year to analyze all the data and decide how to define the boundary between our solar bubble and interstellar space.

Finally, on September 12, 2013, Ed announced their conclusions. Voyager 1, at more than 11 billion miles (18 billion kilometers) from the Sun, had entered interstellar space on August 25, 2012. "In the end, there was general agreement that Voyager 1 was indeed outside in interstellar space," he said.

But it wasn't quite as simple as crossing a finish line. "That location comes with some disclaimers," explained Ed. "We're in a mixed, transitional region of interstellar space. We don't know when we'll reach interstellar space free from the influence of our solar bubble."

In short, as Ed put it, "The path to interstellar space has been a lot more complicated than we imagined."

When Voyager 2 goes interstellar, scientists will know the precise moment because its PLS is still working. Every 190 seconds, the PLS measures the density of the surrounding interstellar plasma. When the density suddenly increases, Voyager 2 will be officially interstellar.

CRUISING THE MAGNETIC HIGHWAY

When scientists first imagined the boundary between the Sun and the stars, they pictured a crossroad formed by opposing magnetic fields. They thought the Sun's magnetic field lines would intersect

with the magnetic field lines from the stars, like two roads in the desert. But that isn't the case at all. It now appears that the magnetic field lines are connected.

Scientists came up with a picture to help explain what they think is going on. Imagine the Sun's magnetic field lines as a highway extending far into space. Like cars traveling along a highway, particles speed away from the Sun on the magnetic field lines. The farther out from the Sun, the fewer the particles. Picture a highway packed with cars. As cars leave the highway, the traffic thins. At some point, all the cars have exited and the highway is empty.

On the magnetic highway, solar particles leave, but the highway is not deserted. Instead, high-energy particles from the stars, called cosmic rays, speed along the highway from the opposite direction. As Voyager 1 cruised along on the magnetic highway, it was surrounded by fewer and fewer solar particles, and more and more cosmic rays.

Scientists think that the magnetic field lines from the Sun merge with the magnetic field lines spiraling through interstellar space. It's like driving on a highway from one state into another: the name of the highway changes, the name of the state changes, but the road is the same. There's one continuous magnetic highway through the solar bubble and into interstellar space. Another big surprise on the journey to the stars.

FREEBIRDS

At some point the Voyagers will be totally interstellar, completely beyond the influence of the Sun. They will be like two birds flying free in the Wild West of space, where the sky is endless and there are no roads. Out of touch with us, never to be heard from again.

Unless . . .

VOYAGER'S ALIEN PLAYLIST

TRACK

8

The year is 1977, and astronomer Frank Drake has an idea. Many of Frank's ideas involve aliens. His Search for Extraterrestrial Intelligence (SETI) began in 1960 when he flashed radio messages to nearby stars in the hope of contacting an intelligent extraterrestrial. He got no response. Frank also came up with the famous Drake Equation, which estimates the number of intelligent civilizations in a galaxy. According to Frank's equation, there could be ten thousand such civilizations in the Milky Way! (But obviously there's proof of only one.)

Frank's newest idea does not involve math or invisible signals. Instead, it is the simple solution to a big question: How do you explain Earth to aliens? Frank Drake's answer is the LP.

Voyager project manager John Casani on August 4, 1977, holding one of the flags that was launched aboard the Voyagers. The Golden Record (left) and its cover (right) are in front of him. Voyager 2 is in the background.

MESSAGE IN A BOTTLE

An LP is a "long-playing" album of music recorded on a 12-inch (30-centimeter) vinyl disk. Grooves corresponding to sound vibrations are etched into the disc, making a recording that is played back when a needle moves in the grooves. LP records spin at 33⅓ revolutions per minute (rpm) on a turntable and usually hold twenty to thirty minutes of music on each side.

Frank figured that an extra-long LP carried aboard the Voyagers could contain a wide variety of sounds and electronic pictures that would introduce extraterrestrials to the planet Earth. If the spin speed were cut in half to 16 2/3 rpm, the record could hold twice as much information as a regular LP.

Carl Sagan loved Frank's idea. He became the chairperson of the Voyager Record Committee, which included Frank and a team of four writers and artists. They had less than six weeks to produce the message that Voyager would carry to the stars.

GOING GOLD

Back in 1977, record albums were selling like crazy. If a record sold 500,000 copies, it was considered a "gold album." By the time Voyager was ready for launch, Fleetwood Mac's album *Rumours* was going gold every two weeks. The Voyager record would also be golden, but "sales" would reach only two.

Rumours and all other vinyl records are pressed from a mold made from a master called a "mother." Mothers are made of copper or nickel. "It seemed ideal to send a mother to the stars," wrote Carl Sagan. "Its resistance to erosion in space would be considerably greater than an ordinary vinyl record's."

Making the mother—two one-sided copper disks bonded together and coated with protective gold—was the easy part. Deciding what to put on it was a different story.

INFINITE PLAYLIST

The makers of the Golden Record debated the playlist. They agreed that ninety minutes of the "best" music from many cultures and times would be included—but what exactly would that be? Chuck Berry, Bach, Beethoven, a Navajo chant, the Chinese folk song "Flowing Streams," and a Peruvian wedding song all were included. The team wanted to include "Here Comes the Sun" by the Beatles, but they couldn't negotiate a deal with the record company.

The team also debated whether they should include pictures that showed both the "best" and "worst" of humanity. War, disease, and poverty are facts of life, but the team decided not to include negative images. It's also a fact that many people pray and often do not agree, but there were no images showing anything religious or political.

Instead, the album contains 116 photographs that reveal the beauty of Earth and its inhabitants. It also includes cheerful greetings spoken in fifty-five languages, as well as recordings of a human heartbeat, a hyena laugh, rumbling thunder, and other "sounds of Earth."

An infinite number of visions of Earth were possible, but only one view could be created. The Golden Record is a time capsule representing a brief moment in the history of humanity and Earth.

On August 20, 1977, just before the launch of Voyager 1, Carl Sagan said, "The spacecraft will be encountered and the record played only if there are advanced spacefaring civilizations in interstellar space. But the launching of this bottle into the cosmic ocean says something very hopeful about life on this planet."

STARMAN

In the center of every vinyl record is a circular sticker with the name of the album, the artist, and the record company. On the Golden Record there's a photo-engraved label with a hand-engraved dedication: "To the makers of music, all worlds, all times."

Each Voyager carries an identical Golden Record. Will one of these mothers ever be played by some alien DJ from another world and time? It's unlikely—but, hey, anything is possible. If by some infinitesimal chance an intelligent extraterrestrial encounters Voyager,

A Golden Record is mounted on the side of each Voyager spacecraft.

ET would remove the Golden Record from the aluminum jacket that has protected it from the interstellar wind for at least a billion years. Then ET would locate the needle and cartridge for playing the record and follow the instructions, written in symbols on the jacket. Upon playing the record, ET would see a written message (recorded as a picture) from Jimmy Carter, president of the United States of America in 1977, on behalf of the "4 billion who inhabit the planet Earth." (It is unlikely ET would know how to read and understand English, but no matter.)

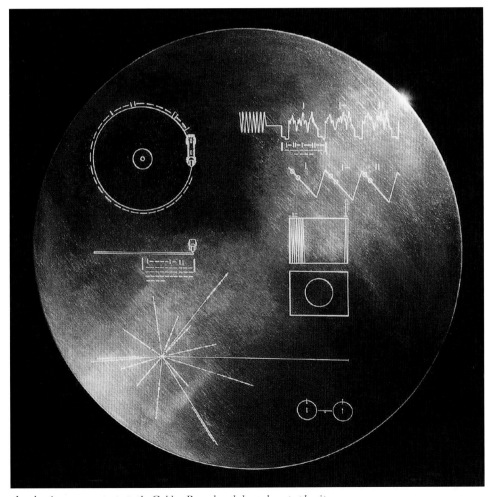

An aluminum cover protects the Golden Record and shows how to play it.

This is a present from a small distant world, a token of our sounds, our science, our images, our music, our thoughts, and our feelings. We are attempting to survive our time so we may live into yours. We hope someday, having solved the problems we face, to join a community of galactic civilizations. This record represents our hope and our determination and our good will in a vast and awesome universe.

ACROSS THE UNIVERSE

The odds of humans from Earth rediscovering the Voyagers are probably greater than the odds of extraterrestrials encountering the spacecraft. After all, we are 100 percent sure that humans exist. In that distant future, space travelers from Earth would encounter the spacecraft, play the Golden Record, and recognize their ancestors from

"Voyager will become our silent ambassador to the stars."—Ed Stone (Image of spiral galaxy NGC 6814 by Hubble Space Telescope, 2016.)

across the universe, who shot a message to the stars. Regardless of their future fate, the Voyagers are both explorers and messengers, representing all of humanity—past, present, and future.

Starting in 2028, power will be cut to the instruments on board, one by one. By the year 2031, all of the spacecraft's scientific equipment will be shut down, but the Voyagers will continue to send signals to Earth. By the year 2050, the Voyagers will be out of range, heading farther and farther into the Milky Way. It will take Voyager 1 forty thousand years to get within 1.6 light-years (9.3 trillion miles or 15 trillion kilometers) of star AC +79 3888, the nearest star on its trajectory. It will take 296,000 years for Voyager 2 to pass within 25 trillion miles (40 trillion kilometers) of Sirius—the brightest star in our sky.

IS THIS THE END?

Although they are traveling 840,000 miles (1.4 million kilometers) per day, deeper and deeper into space, the Voyagers still have years of exploration and discovery ahead of them.

"What we can say is [that] Voyager 1 is bathed in matter from other stars," says Ed Stone. "What we can't say is what exact discoveries await Voyager's continued journey. No one was able to predict all of the details that Voyager 1 has seen. So we expect more surprises."

More than anything else, Voyager has taught us that we cannot accurately predict what exists beyond our limited view. Every place Voyager explored was surprising and different—no two planets were the same, every moon was different from the next, ring systems and stormy weather existed where none were predicted, and there's a magnetic highway to the stars.

So, don't be fooled, beautiful friend. This is not the end. What will the Voyagers "text" home next?

ACKNOWLEDGMENTS

I am very grateful to MIT physics professor John Belcher for reading my manuscript, explaining the science of interstellar space, and making invaluable suggestions and comments. Dr. Belcher is the co-investigator on the Plasma Science Experiment onboard the Voyager Interstellar Mission. Thanks to my son, Sasha Siy, I was introduced to Dr. Belcher's work on Voyager. Sasha was Dr. Belcher's student and advisee at MIT and said Dr. Belcher was "the best physics teacher ever." In 2016 Dr. Belcher was awarded the Hans Christian Oersted Medal of the American Association of Physics Teachers, which is considered the highest teaching award in American physics. I also launch a far-out thanks to Lars Mejnertsen of the Department of Physics of the Imperial College in London, for his exciting image of Neptune's magnetic field. And to Dr. Michael Minovitch: a Jupiter-size thank you for sharing his story of how he invented unlimited, gravity-propelled interplanetary space travel. Finally, much appreciation to Alyssa Mito Pusey, my brilliant, superstar editor, and to artistic designer Diane Earley, who made the book look "smashing."

AUTHOR'S NOTE

I was seventeen back in 1977 when the Voyagers were shot into space. I had no idea. I was too busy listening to my LPs. But if someone had asked me what songs to include on the Golden Record, "Woodstock" by Joni Mitchell would have topped the list. Joni sang about how we are all made of stardust—carbon formed billions of years ago in the hearts of stars. I loved the idea that we are the cosmos.

I grew up listening to vinyl records. The first was a 1964 recording of the Beatles singing "Twist and Shout." I was four years old, dancing in the kitchen. But now that I know what Gary Flandro was doing back in 1964, it blows my mind to think the results of his eureka moment are still playing out today.

It also blows my mind that the eight-track player onboard the Voyagers is still working. How is this possible? There was an eight-track player in my family's Chevy wagon. Before the player broke, we listened to *Sly and the Family Stone's Greatest Hits* over and over. "Everybody Is a Star" would definitely be my next pick for the Golden Record.

Yes! Everybody *is* a star!

When music went digital in the 1980s, I was all grown up. CDs littered the floor of my car, and I still hadn't heard of the Voyagers. Why? Maybe because two unmanned spacecraft dancing around the outer planets couldn't compete with Michael Jackson dancing with zombies in "Thriller"?

I finally discovered the Golden Record in 2005, when I was researching my book *Cars on Mars*. A record album flying in outer space? So cool! Maybe even more amazing than my iPod, which could hold hundreds of songs. During the next few years, I imagined the Voyagers zooming toward the stars as I listened to music while traveling across Canada, Alaska, and the western United States.

In 2012, when I finally landed back in New York State, where I'd grown up, I knew I had to write a book about the Voyagers. Why? Because their story had happened while I was tuned out—doing the twist, listening to music, driving across the country, raising my kids, just living my life. I wanted to go back in time and discover where the Voyagers had been. I wanted to feel the thrill of being flung from planet to planet. I wanted to be with the Voyagers on their epic journey into interstellar space. So I wrote my ticket to the stars.

I've been flying with the Voyagers ever since. And now, so are you.

Alexandra Siy in 1977.

GLOSSARY

ammonia: A strong-smelling, colorless gas made of nitrogen and hydrogen.

asteroid: A small, rocky body that orbits the Sun. Most are in the asteroid belt, between the orbits of Mars and Jupiter.

aurora: Streamers of colored light that appear in the night sky near the poles of a planet. An aurora occurs when particles from the Sun collide with gas in the planet's atmosphere.

Big Bang: The theory of the beginning of the universe, described as a rapid expansion of super-hot, dense matter.

Caltech: California Institute of Technology, located in Pasadena.

carbon: A nonmetallic element that combines with other elements to form organic compounds, which are found in living things.

carbon dioxide: A colorless, odorless gas made of carbon and oxygen.

comet: A mass of ice, dust, and rock that orbits the Sun and displays a glowing tail.

corona: The intensely hot upper atmosphere of the Sun.

coronal mass ejection (CME): A massive, magnetic cloud of plasma that explodes from the Sun's corona and blows into interstellar space.

cosmic rays: High-energy particles that move at near light speed and are composed mostly of protons, electrons, and atomic nuclei that have had their electrons stripped away during their high-speed travel.

Drake Equation: An equation that estimates the number of technologically advanced civilizations in the Milky Way. The equation was invented by Frank Drake in 1961.

eight-track player: An electronic device popular in the 1960s and 1970s that played a cartridge containing eighty minutes of music recorded on magnetic tape.

ethane: An organic compound composed of carbon and hydrogen.

friction: The force exerted on a moving object opposite to its direction of movement. Friction is the result of contact between two surfaces.

gravity: The force of attraction between two bodies.

gravity assist: A technique in which a spacecraft is put into orbit around the Sun or a planet in order to increase the spacecraft's momentum. The massive gravitational attraction of the Sun or the planet causes the spacecraft to speed up, similar to how gravity causes a bike to speed down a hill. When the spacecraft leaves orbit, its increased momentum propels it at high speed toward another planet or out of the solar system.

heliopause: The outermost boundary of the solar system, where the heliosheath ends and interstellar space begins.

heliosheath: The zone between the outer limits of Sun space and the beginning of star space. The inner boundary of the heliosheath is the termination shock, and the outer boundary is the heliopause.

heliosphere: Sun space, or the "bubble" surrounding the solar system as it travels through space. The heliosphere is created by the solar wind streaming off the Sun and pushing back the material (mostly hydrogen and helium gas) from the rest of space.

helium: A colorless, odorless, nonreactive gas.

hertz: A unit used to measure the frequency of sound waves. One hertz (Hz) equals one cycle per second. (A cycle is a wave from beginning to end, before it repeats.)

hydrogen: An extremely reactive, colorless, odorless gas, and the lightest of all the elements.

ice: Any chemical compound that freezes into the solid state at cold temperatures.

interstellar space: The space between the stars. An object is considered to have left Sun space and entered interstellar space when it has moved beyond the heliopause.

interstellar wind: The plasma that blows through interstellar space.

JPL: NASA's Jet Propulsion Laboratory.

LP: The abbreviation for a vinyl "long-playing" phonograph record. An LP includes at least twenty minutes of recorded sound, divided into song tracks, on each side of the record.

magnetic field: The region of space around a magnet, electrical current, or moving charged particle where the force of magnetism is active.

magnetic field lines: The imaginary lines that define the three-dimensional structure of a magnetic field. If a compass needle that is free to turn in any direction is placed in the magnetic field, it will align with the magnetic field lines.

matter: Anything that takes up space, such as a solid, liquid, gas, or plasma.

methane: An organic compound composed of carbon and hydrogen.

Milky Way: Our galaxy, which is made of at least one hundred billion stars, along with enough gas and dust to make billions more, and at least ten times as much dark matter, which cannot be seen.

mother: A grooved metal disk used as a master copy for molding vinyl phonograph records.

NASA: The National Aeronautics and Space Administration.

nitrogen: A colorless, odorless, nonreactive gas.

nuclear reaction: A process in which an atom's nucleus is broken apart or joined (fused) with the nucleus of another atom. Nuclear reactions can release enormous amounts of energy.

orbit: The regular, repeating motion of an object around another object in space.

orbital resonance: The gravitational effect two bodies have on each other as they orbit around a parent body.

organic compounds: Chemicals that contain carbon.

oxygen: A colorless, odorless, reactive gas.

pixel: A dot of colored light that is the smallest unit of an image on a video display.

plasma: A state of matter that is so hot that the atoms are ripped apart, creating a gas of charged particles.

radiation: Energy that speeds through space in the form of particles and waves.

SETI: The Search for Extraterrestrial Intelligence. SETI scientists look for signs of technology that could have been created only by intelligent alien life.

solar flare: An intense burst of light from the Sun.

solar wind: The constant stream of charged particles (plasma) off the Sun.

termination shock: The place where the outgoing solar wind collides with the incoming interstellar wind and suddenly slows down.

track: Originally one song on an LP record, a track is now any song on an album regardless of format.

trajectory: The path of an object moving through space.

UCLA: University of California, Los Angeles.

ultraviolet (UV) rays: Rays of light that have shorter wavelengths than visible light.

velocity: Speed in a given direction.

THE VOYAGERS' GREATEST FINDS

- Auroras on Jupiter, Saturn, and Neptune
- Rings at Jupiter, spokes within Saturn's B ring, braids in Saturn's F ring, two new rings at Uranus, and complete rings around Neptune
- New moons at Jupiter (three), Saturn (three), Uranus (ten), and Neptune (six)
- Volcanoes on Jupiter's moon Io, the most volcanic place in the solar system
- Geysers and atmosphere on Neptune's moon Triton
- Magnetic fields on Uranus and Neptune
- The Great Dark Spot, a big storm system on Neptune

KEEPING UP WITH THE VOYAGERS

Where are the Voyagers right now?:
http://voyager.jpl.nasa.gov/where/

Voyager time line:
http://voyager.jpl.nasa.gov/mission/timeline.html

Interstellar Voyager:
http://www.jpl.nasa.gov/interstellarvoyager/

Interstellar space for kids:
http://spaceplace.nasa.gov/interstellar/en/

Voyager's science instruments:
http://voyager.jpl.nasa.gov/spacecraft/instruments.html

Animation of a gravity assist:
https://www.youtube.com/watch?v=sYp5p2oL51g

"Dance" of Jupiter's moons:
https://www.youtube.com/watch?v=XpsQimYhNkA

Carl Sagan's "Pale Blue Dot" essay:
https://www.youtube.com/watch?v=wupToqz1e2g

Solar flares versus CMEs:
http://www.nasa.gov/content/goddard/the-difference-between-flares-and-cmes

Animation of the magnetic highway:
http://photojournal.jpl.nasa.gov/animation/PIA16486

Motion of the heliosphere:
ftp://space.mit.edu/pub/plasma/models/helio_motion.html

How to play the Golden Record:
http://voyager.jpl.nasa.gov/spacecraft/goldenrec_more.html

"Sounds of Earth" recordings:
http://web.mit.edu/lilybui/www/

Golden Record images:
http://voyager.jpl.nasa.gov/spacecraft/scenes.html

Sounds of space:

http://www-pw.physics.uiowa.edu/space-audio/

Ed Stone on TV:

http://www.cc.com/video-clips/jkirej/the-colbert-report-sign-off

http://www.cc.com/video-clips/g14s8s/the-colbert-report-ed-stone

Voyager photo-essay by *National Geographic*:

http://news.nationalgeographic.com/space/voyager/

Pop-culture and music connections and other interesting stuff:

www.alexandrasiy.com

FURTHER RESOURCES

While researching and writing this book, I read and studied dozens of articles, websites, and books. I highly recommend the following books for advanced readers and teachers:

Bell, Jim. *The Interstellar Age: Inside the Forty-Year Voyager Mission.* New York: Dutton, 2015.

Galilei, Galileo. *Discoveries and Opinions of Galileo.* Translated by Stillman Drake. Garden City, NY: Doubleday, 1957.

Mahon, Basil. *The Man Who Changed Everything: The Life of James Clerk Maxwell.* New York: Wiley, 2003.

Sobel, Dava. *The Planets.* New York: Viking, 2005.

SOURCE NOTES

P. 10: "Who the hell . . . name": John Casani quoted in "Voyager," *National Geographic*, http://news.nationalgeographic.com/space/voyager/.

P. 13: "John . . . enough velocity": Charley Kohlhase quoted in ibid.

P. 17: "It turns . . . doesn't": Ed Stone quoted in Andrew J. Butrica, "Voyager: The Grand Tour of Big Science," in *From Engineering Science to Big Science: The NACA and NASA Collier Trophy Research Project Winners*, ed. Pamela E. Mack (Washington, DC: NASA History Office, 1998), p. 267.

P. 18: "I realized . . . story": ibid., p. 268.

P. 20: "What's that?": Linda A. Morabito, "Discovery of Volcanic Activity on Io: A Historical Review" (Paper, Victor Valley College, Nov. 12, 2012), p. 14.

P. 21: "You'd better . . . crazy!": Peter Kupferman quoted in ibid., p. 28.

P. 23: "There's one . . . imaginations": Ed Stone quoted in Butrica, p. 274.

P. 29: "Over and over . . . figure them out": Ed Stone quoted in Jia-Rui C. Cook, "Saturn Then and Now: 30 Years Since Voyager Visit," JPL, Nov. 11, 2010, http://voyager.jpl.nasa.gov/news/voyager_30_year_saturn.html.

P. 30: "I wanted . . . about it": Candy Hansen, personal communication, July 5, 2016.

P. 33: "curious . . . comet": William Herschel quoted in David Leverington, *Babylon to Voyager and Beyond: A History of Planetary Astronomy* (Cambridge: Cambridge University Press, 2003), p. 150.

P. 36: "We knew . . . surprises": Ed Stone quoted in Elizabeth Landau, "Voyager Mission Celebrates 30 Years Since Uranus," JPL, Jan. 22, 2016, http://voyager.jpl .nasa.gov/news/uranus_30_year.html.

P. 36: "Something . . . screwed up": Heidi Hammel, personal communication, July 5, 2016.

P. 42: "The planet . . . exists": Johann Gottfried Galle quoted in *The Athenaeum* 949 (Oct. 10, 1846): 1046.

P. 49: "Picture of the Century": Michael Norman, "His Head in the Stars," *New York Times Magazine*, May 20, 1990, http://www.nytimes.com/1990/05/20/magazine /his-head-in-the-stars.html?pagewanted=all.

P. 49: "I was . . . turned out": Candy Hansen quoted in "An Alien View of Earth," by Nell Greenfieldboyce, *All Things Considered*, NPR, Feb. 12, 2010, http://www.npr.org/2010/02/12/123614938/an-alien-view-of-earth.

P. 50: "It was . . . incredibly special": ibid.

P. 50: "The point . . . Cosmos": Carl Sagan, "A Pale Blue Dot," *Parade Magazine*, Sept. 9, 1990, p. 52.

P. 54: "No one . . . find": Ed Stone quoted in Jia-Rui C. Cook, "How Do We Know When Voyager Reaches Interstellar Space?" JPL, Sept. 12, 2013, http://www.jpl .nasa.gov/news/news.php?release=2013-278.

P. 54: "Normally . . . later": Ed Stone quoted in "Sun Sends More 'Tsunami Waves' to Voyager 1," JPL, July 7, 2014, http://voyager.jpl.nasa.gov/news/sun_sends_ tsunami.html.

P. 55: "to resonate . . . bell": Ed Stone quoted in "NASA Voyager: 'Tsunami Wave' Still Flies Through Interstellar Space," JPL, Dec. 15, 2014, http://www.jpl.nasa.gov /news/news.php?feature=4411.

Pp. 55–56: "In the end . . . space," "That location . . . solar bubble," and "The path . . . imagined": Ed Stone quoted in Cook, "How Do We Know?"

P. 60: "It seemed . . . record's": Carl Sagan, *Murmurs of Earth: The Voyager Interstellar Record* (New York: Random House, 1978), p. 14.

P. 61: "The spacecraft . . . planet": Carl Sagan quoted in "What Is the Golden Record?," JPL, http://voyager.jpl.nasa.gov/spacecraft/goldenrec.html.

P. 62: "To the makers . . . times": Timothy Ferris, "The Mix Tape of the Gods," *The New York Times*, Sept. 5, 2007, http://www.nytimes.com/2007/09/05/opinion /05ferris.html?_r=0.

Pp. 63–64: "4 billion . . . Earth" and "This is . . . universe": Jimmy Carter, "Voyager Spacecraft Statement by the President," The American Presidency Project, ed. Gerhard Peters and John T. Woolley, July 29, 1977, http://www.presidency.ucsb.edu /ws/?pid=7890.

P. 64: "Voyager will . . . stars": Ed Stone quoted in Tony Phillips, "Voyager Set to Enter Interstellar Space," NASA Science: Science News, Apr. 28, 2011, http://science.nasa.gov/science-news/science-at-nasa/2011/28apr_voyager/.

P. 65: "What we . . . surprises": Ed Stone quoted in Cook, "How Do We Know?"

INDEX

INDEX

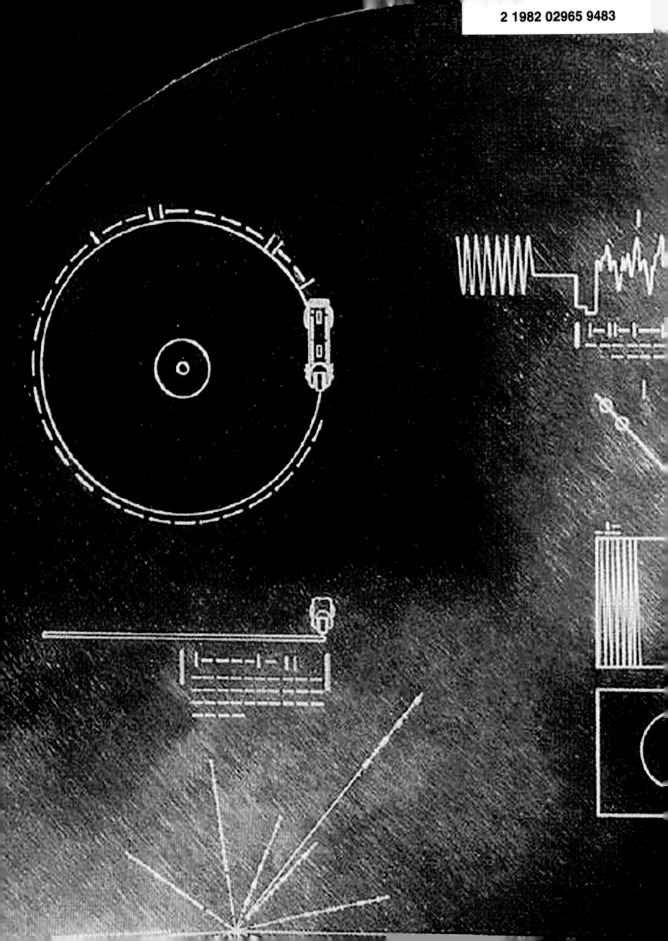